U.S. Fish & Wildlife Service

Casting Beyond the Bow: An Examination of Anglers Fishing From Boats

Addendum to the 2006 National Survey of Fishing, Hunting, and Wildlife-Associated Recreation

Report 2006-9

I0439665

U.S. Fish & Wildlife Service

Casting Beyond the Bow: An Examination of Anglers Fishing From Boats

Addendum to the 2006 National Survey of Fishing, Hunting, and Wildlife-Associated Recreation

Report 2006-9

December 2010

Anna Harris
Wildlife and Sport Fish Restoration Programs
Division of Policy and Programs
U.S. Fish and Wildlife Service
Arlington, VA

This report is intended to complement the National and State Reports for the 2006 National Survey of Fishing, Hunting, and Wildlife-Associated Recreation. The conclusions in this report are the author's and do not represent official positions of the U.S. Fish and Wildlife Service

The author thanks Sylvia Cabrera, Richard Aiken, and Christy Vigfusson for valuable input into this report.

Contents

Introduction

Seventeen million anglers, 16 years of age and older, enjoyed their fishing from a boat in the varied fresh and marine waters of the U.S. in 2006. They spent over 246 million days on the water. This report presents an analysis of their boat use, expenditures, and selected demographic characteristics. For purposes of this report these individuals are referred to as "boaters" and the types of water fished on as either saltwater, Great Lakes, or freshwater (excluding the Great Lakes).

All estimates herein came from the 2006 National Survey of Fishing, Hunting, and Wildlife-Associated Recreation (Survey). The Survey has been conducted since 1955 and is one of the most comprehensive databases on wildlife recreation in the U.S. The focus of the Survey is on anglers, hunters and wildlife watchers—not all outdoor enthusiasts. Therefore, this report only captures fishing from boats—not all recreational boating.[1]

---

[1] According to the National Marine Manufacturers Association there were 66 million adult boaters in 2009 (NMMA. 2009 Recreational Boating Statistical Abstract. Chicago, IL).

Courtesy of Take Me Fishing

Participation and Days by Water Type

All Boaters

Fifty-seven percent of all anglers (17 million people) used a boat to fish in 2006 (Table 1). Forty-eight percent (246 million days) of all fishing days were spent on a boat.

As for the type of fishing, almost three quarters of anglers in the Great Lakes fished from a boat in 2006. Great Lakes anglers also spent the biggest proportion of their time aboard, spending 60% of their fishing days on a boat. Almost 70% of saltwater anglers fished from a boat and more than half of freshwater anglers fished from a boat. Saltwater anglers spent 59% of their fishing days on a boat compared to only 44% of freshwater fishing days spent on a boat.

Courtesy of Take Me Fishing

Table 1. Anglers Fishing From Boats and Days of Participation by Type of Fishing
(Population 16 years old and older. Numbers in thousands)

Participants and days of fishing	Total, all fishing		Freshwater, excludes Great Lakes		Great Lakes		Saltwater	
	Number	Percent	Number	Percent	Number	Percent	Number	Percent
Total anglers	29,952	100	25,035	100	1,420	100	7,717	100
Anglers fishing from boats	17,035	57	13,073	52	1,054	74	5,304	69
Total days of fishing	516,781	100	419,942	100	18,016	100	85,663	100
Days fishing from boats	246,038	48	185,074	44	10,728	60	50,236	59

Note: Detail does not add to total because of multiple responses and nonresponses.

Freshwater Boaters

A state-by-state analysis of freshwater boaters reveals that Minnesota, which prides itself on being the "Land of 10,000 Lakes," has the largest number of boaters and the highest percent of freshwater anglers fishing from boats (Table 2).

Wisconsin has the second largest number of freshwater boaters (885 thousand) while Florida ranks third in participation with 836 thousand boaters. Seventy-nine percent of freshwater anglers in Minnesota fished from boats, followed closely by Wisconsin (71%) and Michigan (70%). There are nine states where boat use by freshwater anglers is 60% or higher (Alabama, Arkansas, Maine, Michigan, Minnesota, New Hampshire, South Carolina, South Dakota, and Wisconsin).

Table 2. Freshwater Anglers and Boaters by State Where Fishing Occurred
(Population 16 years old and older. Numbers in thousands)

	Anglers	Boaters	Percent
US Total	**25,035**	**13,073**	**52**
Alaska	191	91	48
Alabama	714	465	65
Arkansas	655	403	62
Arizona	422	195	46
California	1,224	620	51
Colorado	660	166	25
Connecticut	204	85	42
Delaware	58	31	54
Florida	1,417	836	59
Georgia	1,025	559	54
Hawaii	22	...	...
Iowa	438	193	44
Idaho	350	164	47
Illinois	777	359	46
Indiana	677	311	46
Kansas	404	168	42
Kentucky	721	321	44
Louisiana	549	324	59
Massachusetts	292	133	45
Maryland	364	142	39
Maine	303	204	67
Michigan	1,192	828	70
Minnesota	1,381	1,086	79
Missouri	1,076	535	50
Mississippi	508	253	50
Montana	291	148	51
North Carolina	884	362	41
North Dakota	106	60	56
Nebraska	198	69	35
New Hampshire	198	125	63
New Jersey	243	128	53
New Mexico	248	52	21
Nevada	142	49	35
New York	741	344	46
Ohio	982	275	28
Oklahoma	611	318	52
Oregon	491	253	52
Pennsylvania	914	434	48
Rhode Island	50	24	49
South Carolina	612	386	63
South Dakota	135	83	62
Tennessee	871	463	53
Texas	1,860	696	37
Utah	375	172	46
Virginia	622	303	49
Vermont	114	64	56
Washington	538	308	57
Wisconsin	1,253	885	71
West Virginia	376	98	26
Wyoming	203	81	40

... Sample size too small to report data reliably.
Note: Detail does not add to total because of multiple response and nonresponses.

Anglers spent a total of 185 million days aboard a boat in freshwater, with an average of 13 days fishing from boats (Table 3).

There were 16 states with above average days (Alabama, Arkansas, Connecticut, Delaware, Florida, Georgia, Louisiana, Massachusetts, Michigan, Minnesota, Missouri, Mississippi, Oklahoma, South Carolina, Tennessee, and Texas). Massachusetts and Alabama tied with the highest average of 18 days. Florida followed closely with an average of 17 days spent boating in freshwater. Alaska had the lowest freshwater boating days with an average of 6 days.

Table 3. Days Freshwater Fishing From a Boat by State Where Fishing Occurred
(Population 16 years old and older. Numbers in thousands)

	Days Fishing from Boats	Average Days Boating
US Total	185,074	13
Alaska	569	6
Alabama	8,196	18
Arkansas	5,842	15
Arizona	1,995	10
California	4,266	7
Colorado	1,591	10
Connecticut	1,234	14
Delaware	453	14
Florida	13,903	17
Georgia	8,139	15
Hawaii	...	...
Iowa	1,913	10
Idaho	1,759	11
Illinois	4,749	13
Indiana	3,421	11
Kansas	1,709	10
Kentucky	2,873	9
Louisiana	4,471	14
Massachusetts	2,383	18
Maryland	1,369	10
Maine	1,771	9
Michigan	11,470	14
Minnesota	16,384	15
Missouri	7,409	14
Mississippi	3,935	16
Montana	1,033	7
North Carolina	3,931	11
North Dakota	431	7
Nebraska	909	13
New Hampshire	1,294	10
New Jersey	1,569	12
New Mexico	373	7
Nevada	339	7
New York	2,776	8
Ohio	2,660	10
Oklahoma	4,547	15
Oregon	2,257	9
Pennsylvania	5,654	13
Rhode Island	252	10
South Carolina	5,784	15
South Dakota	703	8
Tennessee	7,437	16
Texas	10,810	16
Utah	1,120	7
Virginia	2,933	10
Vermont	507	8
Washington	3,312	11
Wisconsin	10,843	12
West Virginia	1,071	11
Wyoming	610	8

... Sample size too small to report data reliably.

Figure 1. Average Days Freshwater Anglers Fish From a Boat

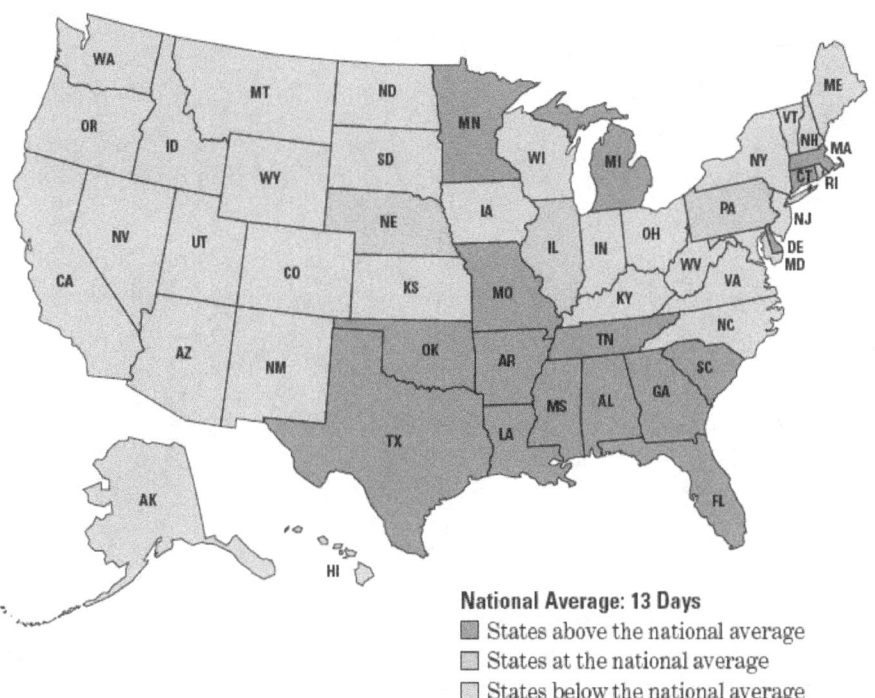

National Average: 13 Days
- States above the national average
- States at the national average
- States below the national average

Courtesy of Take Me Fishing

Saltwater Boaters

Saltwater anglers' boating participation ranged from 90% in Alaska to 48% in North Carolina (Table 4).

Over 80% of saltwater anglers in Louisiana and New Jersey used a boat in 2006. In terms of participation, Florida has the most saltwater boaters with over 1.5 million.

Table 4. Saltwater Anglers and Boaters by State Where Fishing Occurred
(Population 16 years old and older. Numbers in thousands)

	Anglers	Boaters	Percent
US Total	7,717	5,304	69
Alaska	180	162	90
Alabama	153	94	62
California	761	542	71
Connecticut	157	101	65
Delaware	117	70	60
Florida	2,002	1,513	76
Georgia	146	*84	*57
Hawaii	154	86	56
Louisiana	289	245	84
Massachusetts	298	204	69
Maryland	372	291	78
Maine	100	49	49
Mississippi	*66	*37	*57
North Carolina	519	250	48
New Hampshire	47	32	69
New Jersey	496	408	82
New York	291	221	76
Oregon	150	109	72
Rhode Island	122	82	67
South Carolina	325	181	56
Texas	1,147	633	55
Virginia	352	256	73
Washington	286	186	65

*Estimate based on a sample size of 10–29.
Note: Detail does not add to total because of multiple response and nonresponses.

Saltwater anglers spent 50 million days fishing from boats in 2006 (Table 5).

Nationally, anglers spent on average 9 days boating in saltwater. Seven states had higher average days than the U.S. total (Connecticut, Georgia, Louisiana, Massachusetts, Mississippi, New York and Texas). New Hampshire, the state with the shortest ocean coastline of any U.S. coastal state, had the lowest average of 3 days spent fishing from a boat in saltwater.

Table 5. Days Saltwater Fishing From a Boat by State Where Fishing Occurred
(Population 16 years old and older. Numbers in Thousands)

	Days Fishing from Boats	Average Days Boating
US Total	50,236	9
Alaska	788	5
Alabama	346	4
California	4,977	9
Connecticut	1,082	11
Delaware	360	5
Florida	13,783	9
Georgia	*1,239	*15
Hawaii	481	6
Louisiana	2,503	10
Massachusetts	2,186	11
Maryland	2,318	8
Maine	315	6
Mississippi	*449	*12
North Carolina	1,519	6
New Hampshire	107	3
New Jersey	3,629	9
New York	2,722	13
Oregon	569	5
Rhode Island	606	7
South Carolina	1,351	8
Texas	6,033	10
Virginia	1,783	7
Washington	1,091	6

*Estimate based on a sample size of 10–29.

Figure 2. Average Days Saltwater Anglers Fish From a Boat

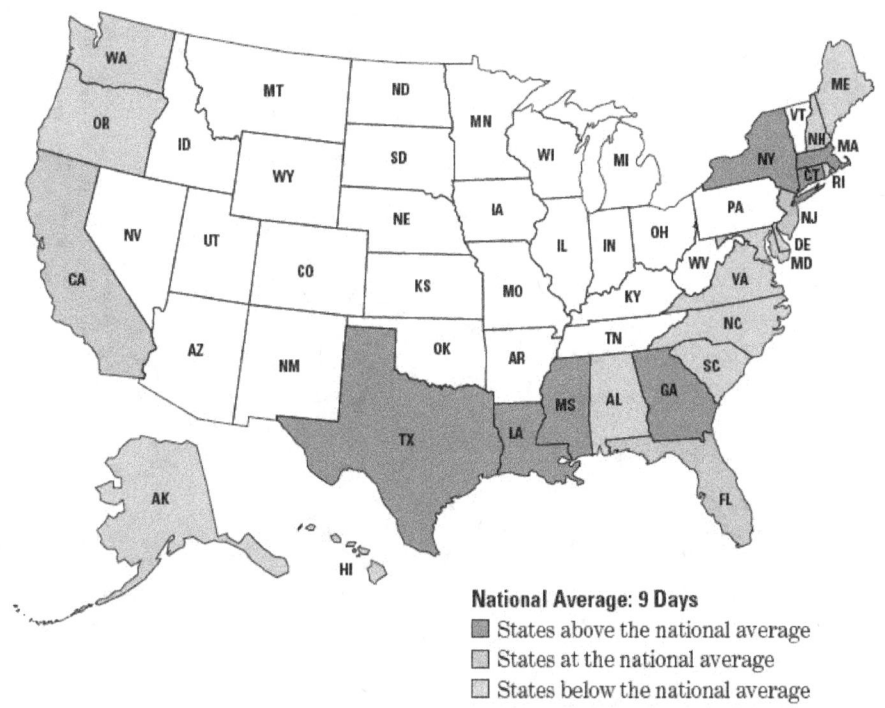

National Average: 9 Days

■ States above the national average
■ States at the national average
□ States below the national average

Great Lakes Boaters

Seventy-four percent of all anglers in the Great Lakes used a boat to fish during 2006 (Table 6).

In the Great Lake states, Indiana had the highest reportable boater participation with 89% of its anglers fishing from a boat, Ohio anglers used boats 80% of the time and Illinois ranked third with 77%. Michigan had the largest number of boaters in the Great Lakes (350 thousand).

The days anglers spent fishing from boats in the Great Lakes totaled 10.7 million in 2006 (Table 7). The average number of days spent fishing from a boat in the Great Lakes was 10. Michigan had the largest number of days (4.3 million) while Indiana had the highest average days anglers fished from a boat (17 days).

Table 6. Great Lakes Anglers and Boaters by State Where Fishing Occurred
(Population 16 years old and older. Numbers in thousands)

	Anglers	Boaters	Percent
US Total	**1,420**	**1,054**	**74**
Illinois	*56	*43	*77
Indiana	*46	*41	*89
Michigan	461	350	76
Minnesota	*48	...	...
New York	247	157	64
Ohio	328	263	80
Pennsylvania	*85	*47	*55
Wisconsin	235	164	70

*Estimate based on a sample size of 10–29.
... Sample size too small to report data reliably.
Note: Detail does not add to total because of multiple response and nonresponses.

Table 7. Days Great Lakes Fishing From a Boat by State Where Fishing Occurred
(Population 16 years old and older. Numbers in thousands)

	Days Fishing from Boats	Average Days Boating
US Total	**10,728**	**10**
Illinois	*292	*7
Indiana	*667	*17
Michigan	4,318	13
Minnesota	...	...
New York	1,269	8
Ohio	1,959	7
Pennsylvania	*297	*6
Wisconsin	1,671	10

*Estimate based on a sample size of 10–29.
... Sample size too small to report data reliably.

Figure 3. Average Days Great Lakes Anglers Fish From a Boat

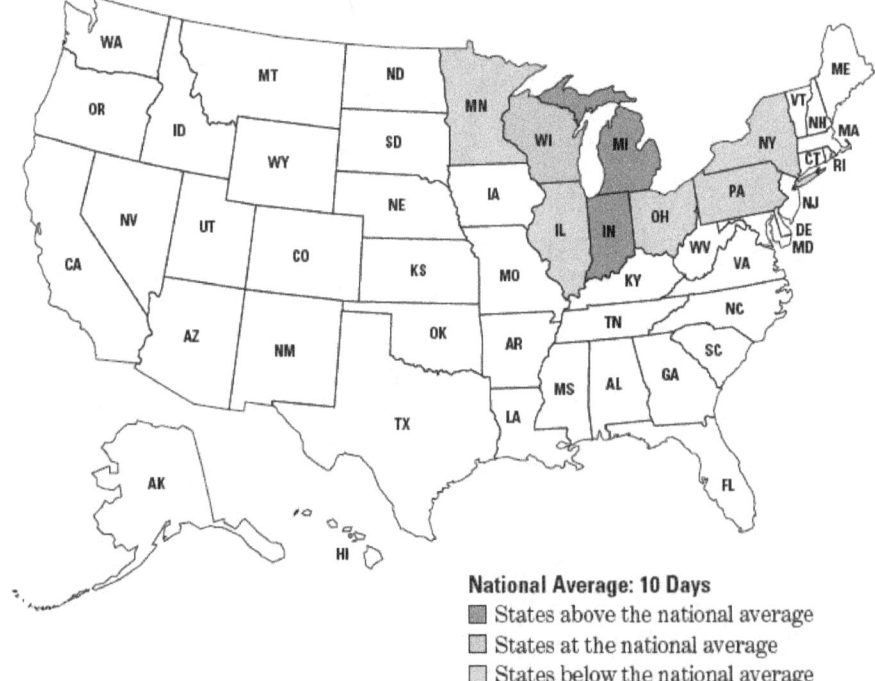

National Average: 10 Days
- States above the national average
- States at the national average
- States below the national average

Boater Demographics

The South Atlantic has the largest population and the most anglers (Table 8). An examination of boaters by water type reveals that the East North Central region has the highest participation of freshwater boaters. Since it is where the Great Lakes are located, it also has the most anglers fishing from boats in those lakes. For saltwater boaters, the South Atlantic had more than double the number of boaters of any other region with almost 2 million participants.

Fifty-two percent of the U.S. population is female. For all anglers, this figure drops to 25%. When comparing these figures to boating anglers the type of fishing that has the highest proportion of female boaters is freshwater (22%). Twenty percent of all saltwater boaters were female. In the Great Lakes, females represent 17% of all boaters. Boating follows the trend of all fishing and continues to be a male dominated sport.

In 2006 20% of the U.S. population was between 35 and 44 years old and this percentage was even higher for anglers (25%). Angling boaters followed suit; with a quarter or more between the ages of 35 to 44 years old. Freshwater boating appealed to young and old alike—11% were 16 to 24 years old and 10% were 65 years old or older. Thirty percent of Great Lakes boaters were 55 years old or older compared to only 25% of all anglers.

Seventy-seven percent of the U.S. population lives in an urban area.[2] Anglers are less likely to live in urban areas. Freshwater angling boaters are least likely to live in an urban area (57%),

Courtesy of Take Me Fishing

while 74% of all saltwater angling boaters do. Sixty-five percent of boaters in the Great Lakes live in urban areas.

Eighty-five percent of American's had completed 12 years of schooling or more in 2006. Anglers followed a similar educational pattern as the general public. Saltwater boaters were the most educated anglers with 34% completing 4 years of college or more. Twenty-six percent of freshwater boaters had completed 4 years or more of college compared to 30% of boaters in the Great Lakes.

Boats can cost as little as $50 for a used kayak to over $30,000 for a premier bass boat. Anglers and boaters alike come from higher income households when compared to the total U.S. population. Forty-six percent of saltwater boating anglers came from households earning $75 thousand or more, as did 38% of Great Lakes boating anglers and 32% of freshwater boating anglers. They are all higher than the U.S. population's 22%.

[2] Urban is defined as all territory, population, and housing units located within boundaries that encompass densely settled territory, consisting of core census block groups or blocks that have a population density of at least 1,000 people per square mile and surrounding census blocks that have an overall density of at least 500 people per square mile. See <http://www.census.gov/geo/www/ua/urbanruralclass.html> for more detailed information.

Table 8. Boater Demographics
(Population 16 years old and older; Numbers in thousands)

	U.S. Population	Percent	Total, All Anglers	Percent	Freshwater Boaters	Percent	Great Lakes Boaters	Percent	Saltwater Boaters	Percent
Total Persons	229,245	100	29,952	100	13,073	100	1,054	100	5,304	100
Census Geographic Division										
New England	11,233	5	1,246	4	520	4	NA	NA	400	8
Middle Atlantic	31,518	14	2,550	9	845	6	*193	*19	703	13
East North Central	35,609	16	5,190	17	2,534	19	738	74	NA	NA
West North Central	15,458	7	3,284	11	1,909	15	*66	*7	NA	NA
South Atlantic	43,965	19	6,116	20	2,407	18	NA	NA	1,961	37
East South Central	13,722	6	2,436	8	1,240	9	NA	NA	209	4
West South Central	25,407	11	3,952	13	1,491	11	NA	NA	848	16
Mountain	15,651	7	2,084	7	903	7	NA	NA	NA	NA
Pacific	36,681	16	3,094	10	1,225	10	NA	NA	875	16
Gender										
Males	110,273	48	22,337	75	10,202	78	874	83	4,233	80
Females	118,972	52	7,615	25	2,871	22	180	17	1,070	20
Age										
16-17	8,272	4	1,103	4	453	3	...	...	128	2
18-24	23,292	10	2,406	8	1,046	8	*76	*7	311	6
25-34	37,468	16	4,857	16	2,179	17	*160	*15	856	16
35-44	45,112	20	7,476	25	3,095	24	288	27	1,360	26
45-54	44,209	19	6,647	22	2,771	21	188	18	1,284	24
55-64	32,867	14	4,616	15	2,190	17	240	23	875	17
65+	38,024	17	2,847	10	1,339	10	*78	*7	489	9
Population Density										
Urban	176,740	77	18,303	61	7,364	57	690	65	3,787	74
Rural	52,504	23	11,649	39	5,466	43	364	35	1,333	26
Education										
0–11 years	34,621	15	4,040	13	1,607	12	*95	*9	431	8
12 years	78,073	34	10,266	34	4,545	35	352	33	1,603	30
1–3 yrs of college	53,019	23	7,590	25	3,474	27	289	27	1,443	27
4 years of college	39,506	17	5,115	17	2,271	17	209	20	1,173	22
5 yrs + of college	24,025	10	2,941	10	1,177	10	110	10	655	12
Income										
Under $20,000	26,046	12	2,113	7	742	6	...	...	98	2
$20-$29,999	21,898	10	2,746	10	989	9	...	...	288	5
$30-$39,999	21,510	10	3,053	10	1,387	10	...	...	333	6
$40-$49,999	17,699	8	2,766	9	1,142	9	105	11	473	9
$50-$74,999	33,434	15	5,981	20	2,889	22	278	30	991	19
$75-$99,999	21,519	9	4,074	14	1,853	14	192	20	931	18
$100,000 or More	29,159	13	5,167	17	2,306	18	166	18	1,487	28
Not Reported	57,981	25	4,051	14	1,764	14	123	13	666	13

*Estimate based on a sample size of 10–29.   ... Sample size too small to report data reliably.   Note: Detail does not add to total because of multiple response and nonresponses.

Boat Type, Length, and Completion of Boater Safety Course

Three-fourths of the earth's surface is water and what better way to enjoy it than maneuvering around in a canoe, jon boat, yacht, or sailboat. One of the most important decisions a boater can make is deciding what kind of boat to buy or rent. This depends on a number of factors including distance to the water, what kind of water, and conditions of the water body. Table 9 provides a breakdown of boaters using motor and non-motor boats to fish by water type as well as the length of boat used most often.

Saltwater boaters were more likely to use motorboats (81%) compared to Great Lakes (79%) and freshwater (71%) boaters. A quarter of freshwater boaters used something other than a motorboat, like a canoe or kayak, when fishing. It's difficult to judge what kind of boat is being used by just looking at two categories of motor and non-motor boats. Therefore, in 2006, the information on boating was expanded to include length of boat used and participation in a boater safety course.

We have seen already that saltwater anglers were more likely to use a motorboat and in Table 9 we also find that saltwater anglers were the primary users of boats over 40 feet long. Nine percent of saltwater boaters fished from a boat 41 feet long or longer while only one percent of freshwater boaters fished from a boat larger than 40 feet. The most popular length for freshwater boaters was a boat between 13 and 16 feet long. Thirty-three percent of freshwater boaters were fishing from this type of vessel. As for Great Lakes boaters, 28% were fishing from boats 20 to 25 feet long.

Even though you're safer on the water than the road, accidents on the water can happen and they can be hazardous. There are some simple precautions to help avoid these accidents, one of which is participation in a boater safety course. Boater safety courses often cover topics like navigation rules and regulations, vessel length and capacity, registration information, and personal watercraft basics. It's not surprising that saltwater boaters, who use the larger vessels, had the highest boater safety course completion rate of 29% in 2006. Less than 20% of freshwater anglers completed a boater safety course while 27% of Great Lakes boaters completed one. This still leaves a large majority of those on the water who have not completed a boater safety course.

Table 9. Boat Type, Length and Completion of Boater Safety Course
(Population 16 years old and older. Numbers in thousands)

	Freshwater		Great Lakes		Saltwater	
	Boaters	*Percent*	*Boaters*	*Percent*	*Boaters*	*Percent*
Fishing from Motorboats and Nonmotorboats						
Total Boaters	13,073	100	1,054	100	5,304	100
Motorboat	9,257	71	828	79	4,315	81
Non-Motorboat	3,247	25	195	19	666	13
Length of Boat Used Most Often						
Less than 13 feet	2,043	16	*102	*10	418	8
13 to 16 feet	4,362	33	215	20	748	14
17 to 19 feet	2,877	22	261	25	847	16
20 to 25 feet	2,000	15	292	28	1,438	27
26 to 30 feet	336	3	*70	*7	439	8
31 to 40 feet	109	1	*47	*4	362	7
41 feet or more	90	1	...	...	457	9
Completing a Boater Safety Course						
Completed course	2,402	18	284	27	1,518	29
Did not complete or attempt course	10,322	79	755	72	3,599	68

*Estimate based on a sample size of 10–29.
... Sample size too small to report data reliably.
Note: Detail does not add to total because some people who fished from a boat did not own a boat and because of multiple responses and nonresponses.

Who Boaters Take Fishing and What Information They Need

Anglers Fishing Alone or with Others

Fishing from a boat can be enjoyed with friends, family or in the solitude of one's own company. Eight percent of freshwater anglers enjoyed the latter, preferring to boat alone in 2006. This compares to 6% of Great Lake boaters and 5% of saltwater boaters (Table 10).

In all three water types, friends are the most popular group boaters fish with. It was also common for boaters to bring spouses and other family members out fishing. Spouses or partners accompanied 21% of boaters in freshwater, 15% of Great Lakes boaters and 18% of saltwater boaters.

Types of Information Boaters Need

The types of information boaters looked for and the sources that were helpful to find this information are presented in Table 11.

The most popular type of information boaters looked for was on fish species (Table 11). Information on weather conditions was also important, especially for those saltwater fishing. Around 13% of boaters were looking for information on fishing rules and regulations. Eleven percent of saltwater and Great Lakes boaters needed directions to fishing sites compared to 10% of freshwater boaters.

Sources of Boating Information

To find helpful information, boaters relied on a variety of sources (Table 11). The most popular source of information was family, friends and other anglers or boaters. The internet was another popular source for information. Fifteen percent of boaters in the Great Lakes went online to find helpful information compared to 14% for saltwater boaters and 12% for freshwater boaters. Between 8 and 10 percent boaters found helpful information from TV or radio shows. Another 8% found bait and tackle shops provided helpful information (9% for Great Lakes boaters). Saltwater boaters were more likely to acquire information from magazines and newspapers compared to freshwater and Great Lakes boaters. Call-in service centers appear to be a thing of the past. Only 1% of freshwater and saltwater anglers found helpful boating information from this source.

Sources of Boating Information By Age

Helpful sources of information may also differ by a boater's age. One would expect to find a higher internet use by younger boaters who are more likely to own a computer and have access to the internet. Table 12 reinforces this theory.[3]

Finding helpful boating information on the internet was highest for 25 to 34-year-olds (12%). Only 5% of those 65 years old or older found helpful boating information off the internet. Those 65 and older find helpful information from TV or radio sources 10% of the time. Sixty-four-year-olds are the most frequent users of bait and tackle shops for helpful information. Family, friends, and other anglers or boaters are still the most popular sources of information for all age categories.

---

[3] The percents in Table 12 are the number of angling boaters in all water types, in each age category, who reported using each source of information divided by the total number of angling boaters. A boater could have answered using more than one source of information.

Table 10. Anglers Fishing Most Often From Boats Alone or With Others
(Population 16 years old and older. Numbers in thousands)

Fishing Alone or With Others	Freshwater		Great Lakes		Saltwater	
	Boaters	Percent	Boaters	Percent	Boaters	Percent
Fished most often alone	1,593	8	*88	*6	402	5
Fished most often with friends	5,643	30	576	38	2,933	37
Fished most often with spouse/partner	4,001	21	224	15	1,410	18
Fished most often with children	2,961	16	173	11	1,153	15
Fished most often with parents	1,207	6	*143	*9	512	7
Fished most often with other family	3,021	16	325	21	1,155	15
Fished most often with other	366	2	...	...	298	4

*Estimate based on a sample size of 10–29.
... Sample size too small to report data reliably.

Table 11. Information Used by Anglers Fishing from Boats
(Population 16 years old and older. Numbers in thousands)

Types of Information	Freshwater Boaters	Freshwater Percent	Great Lakes Boaters	Great Lakes Percent	Saltwater Boaters	Saltwater Percent
Directions to boat launch	1,007	7	*108	*8	404	6
Directions to fishing sites	1,471	10	146	11	739	11
Boating rules and regulations	1,295	9	*108	*8	514	8
Fishing rules and regulations	2,102	14	163	12	904	13
Water attributes (e.g., depth)	1,557	11	164	12	578	9
Fish species	3,530	24	349	25	1,579	23
Weather conditions	2,853	19	303	22	1,619	24
Other	381	3	...	...	221	3
None	621	4	*52	*4	238	4
Sources of Information						
Published boat guide	736	4	*88	*6	433	6
Internet	2,083	12	236	15	1,066	14
TV or radio	1,380	8	136	9	816	10
Call-in service center	160	1	...	...	*62	*1
State fish and game agency	1,213	7	*75	*5	350	4
Magazines and newspapers	1,080	6	*77	*5	570	7
Boating, fishing, outdoors shows	281	2	*62	*4	138	2
Friends, family, other anglers/boaters	3,471	19	328	21	1,504	19
Bait and tackle shop	1,394	8	138	9	649	8
Other	805	5	*75	*5	407	5
None	5,197	29	354	23	1,828	23

*Estimate based on a sample size of 10–29.
... Sample size too small to report data reliably.
Note: Detail does not add to total because of multiple response and nonresponses.

Table 12. Sources of Information Used by Anglers Fishing from Boats by Age
(Population 16 years old and older)

Sources of Information (percent)	16–17	18–24	25–34	35–44	45–54	55–64	65+
Published boat guide	...	*1	3	4	4	6	5
Internet	*5	7	12	10	10	10	5
TV or radio	*5	4	6	5	6	9	10
Call-in service center	...	...	...	*1	*1	*1	...
State fish and game agency	...	*3	4	5	5	6	5
Magazines and newspapers	*2	*3	4	4	6	6	8
Boating, fishing, outdoors shows	...	...	*1	*1	1	2	*1
Friends, family, other anglers/boaters	12	14	15	13	16	19	17
Bait and tackle shop	*3	6	5	6	7	8	6
Other	*4	*3	3	3	4	4	5
None	27	22	23	22	20	22	23

*Estimate based on a sample size of 10–29.
... Sample size too small to report data reliably.

Boat Launches

A boat launch is a popular way for boaters to access the water. Fifty-eight percent of both freshwater and Great Lakes boaters used a boat launch on at least one of their fishing trips in 2006. Saltwater boaters were less likely to access a boat launch, with 46% using them.

When a saltwater boater did access a boat launch, they stayed close to home with 26% traveling 5 miles or less to their preferred launch (Table 13). Great Lakes and freshwater boaters either traveled a relatively short distance or a very long distance to access a boat launch. Forty percent of Great Lakes boaters traveled 20 miles or less to the boat launch they used most often while another 17% hauled their boats 101 miles or more to their preferred launches. Forty-four percent of freshwater boaters traveled 20 miles or less to reach their preferred boat launch. Another 16% traveled over 100 miles to reach the launch they used most often.

USFWS

Table 13. Boat Launches Used by Anglers
(Population 16 years old and older. Numbers in thousands)

	Freshwater		Great Lakes		Saltwater	
	Boaters	Percent	Boaters	Percent	Boaters	Percent
Total Boaters	**13,073**	**100**	**1,054**	**100**	**5,304**	**100**
Used a boat launch	7,601	58	615	58	2,461	46
Did not use a boat launch	5,472	42	439	42	2,842	54
Distance to Boat Launch Used Most Often						
5 Miles or less	1,244	16	*92	*15	632	26
6 to 20 miles	2,103	28	*156	*25	634	26
21 to 40 miles	1,337	18	*52	*8	352	14
41 to 75 miles	1,050	14	*52	*8	323	13
76 to 100 miles	441	6	...	...	151	6
101 miles or more	1,208	16	105	17	335	14

*Estimate based on a sample size of 10–29.
... Sample size too small to report data reliably.
Note: Detail does not add to total because of multiple response and nonresponses.

State-by-State Launch Use

A state-by-state breakdown provides more information about who is accessing boat launches.

Nationally, 58% of all freshwater anglers who fished from a boat used a boat launch to access the water (Table 14). While North Dakota topped this at 83%, another ten states also had more than 58% of their freshwater anglers using boat launches (Arizona, Iowa, Montana, North Dakota, New Mexico, Oklahoma, Oregon, South Carolina, South Dakota, Tennessee, Utah, and Washington).

Table 14. Launch Usage by Freshwater Boaters

(Population 16 years old and older. Numbers in thousands)

	Boaters	Used a Boat Launch	Percent
US Total	**13,073**	**7,601**	**58**
Alaska	91	43	48
Alabama	465	265	57
Arkansas	403	166	41
Arizona	195	117	60
California	620	253	41
Colorado	166	81	48
Connecticut	85	46	54
Delaware	31	*7	*23
Florida	836	473	57
Georgia	559	172	31
Hawaii	...	...	...
Iowa	193	117	60
Idaho	164	92	56
Illinois	359	208	58
Indiana	311	168	54
Kansas	168	71	42
Kentucky	321	169	53
Louisiana	324	181	56
Massachusetts	133	52	39
Maryland	142	63	44
Maine	204	87	43
Michigan	828	412	50
Minnesota	1,086	584	54
Missouri	535	288	54
Mississippi	253	136	54
Montana	148	90	61
North Carolina	362	165	46
North Dakota	60	49	83
Nebraska	69	32	46
New Hampshire	125	36	28
New Jersey	128	53	41
New Mexico	52	*34	*65
Nevada	49	*22	*45
New York	344	*116	*34
Ohio	275	134	49
Oklahoma	318	214	67
Oregon	253	169	67
Pennsylvania	434	218	50
Rhode Island	24	*9	*35
South Carolina	386	227	59
South Dakota	83	54	64
Tennessee	463	303	65
Texas	696	388	56
Utah	172	118	68
Virginia	303	128	42
Vermont	64	18	28
Washington	308	199	65
Wisconsin	885	483	55
West Virginia	98	*45	*46
Wyoming	81	40	50

*Estimate based on a sample size of 10–29.
... Sample size too small to report data reliably.
Note: Detail does not add to total because of multiple response and nonresponses.

Figure 4. Percent of Launch Usage by Freshwater Boaters

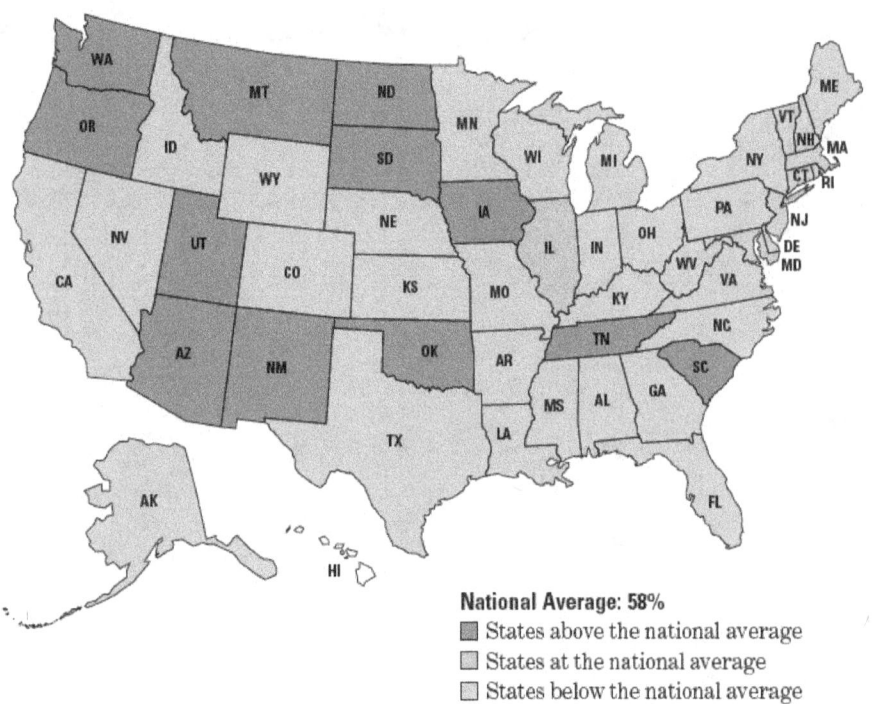

National Average: 58%
- States above the national average
- States at the national average
- States below the national average

Courtesy of Take Me Fishing

Saltwater boaters were, on average, the least likely to access a boat launch. Table 15 reveals there is a lot of variability in boat launch usage by state, ranging from a high of 78% in Georgia to a low of 15% in Rhode Island.[4] Coastal Georgia, Texas, and Mississippi had the highest boat launch usage by saltwater anglers.

---

[4] Because of the small sample size, use these results with caution.

Table 15. Launch Usage by Saltwater Boaters
(Population 16 years old and older. Numbers in thousands)

	Boaters	Used a Boat Launch	Percent
US Total	**5,304**	**2,461**	**46**
Alaska	162	36	22
Alabama	94	*45	*48
California	542	153	28
Connecticut	101	46	45
Delaware	70	16	23
Florida	1,513	545	36
Georgia	*84	*66	*78
Hawaii	86	18	21
Louisiana	245	142	58
Massachusetts	204	57	28
Maryland	291	99	34
Maine	49	*24	*50
Mississippi	*37	*26	*68
North Carolina	250	*65	*26
New Hampshire	32	*8	*26
New Jersey	408	80	20
New York	221	*40	*18
Oregon	109	63	58
Rhode Island	82	*12	*15
South Carolina	181	69	38
Texas	633	484	76
Virginia	256	123	48
Washington	186	118	63

*Estimate based on a sample size of 10–29.
... Sample size too small to report data reliably.
Note: Detail does not add to total because of multiple response and nonresponses.

Figure 5. Percent of Launch Usage by Saltwater Boaters

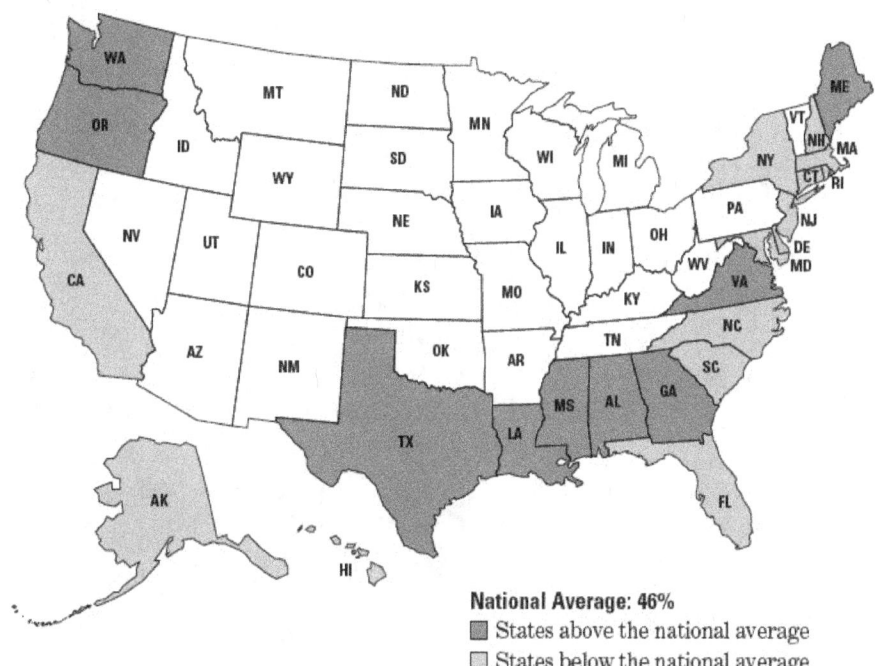

National Average: 46%
■ States above the national average
□ States below the national average

Fifty-eight percent of boaters in the Great Lakes accessed a boat launch at least once during a fishing trip in 2006 (Table 16). Indiana had the highest usage rate with 68% of boaters using a boat launch.

Table 16. Launch Usage by Great Lakes Boaters
(Population 16 years old and older. Numbers in thousands)

	Boaters	Used a Boat Launch	Percent
US Total	**1,054**	**615**	**58**
Illinois	43	…	…
Indiana*	41	28	68
Michigan	350	221	63
Minnesota	…	…	…
New York*	157	87	55
Ohio*	263	127	48
Pennsylvania	47	…	…
Wisconsin*	164	65	40

*States where estimates are based on sample sizes between 10 and 29.
… Sample size too small to report data reliably.
Note: Detail does not add to total because of multiple response and nonresponses.

Figure 6. Percent of Launch Usage by Great Lakes Boaters

National Average: 58%
■ States above the national average
■ States below the national average

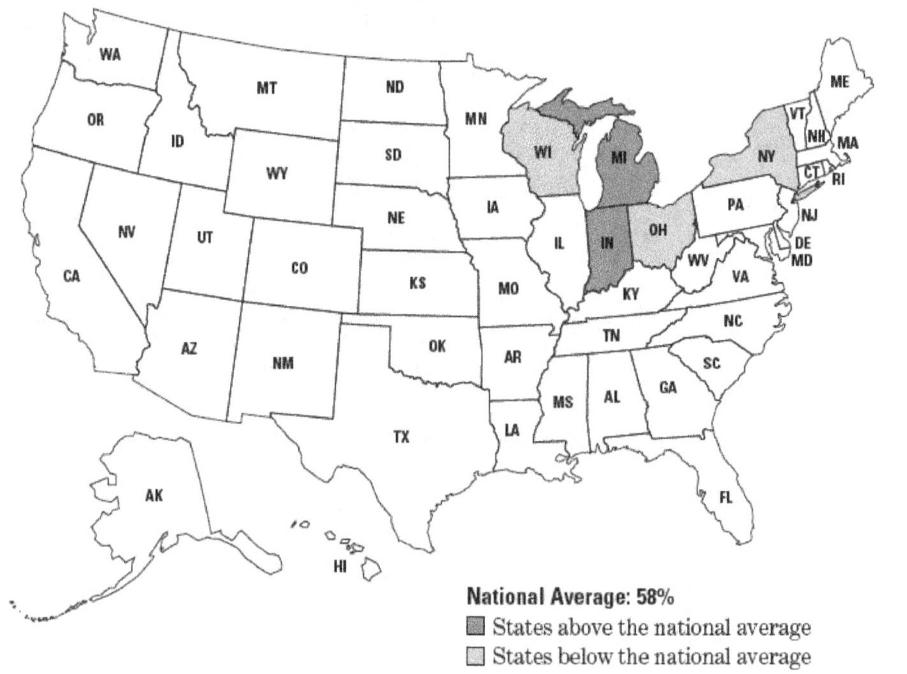

Launch Facility Improvement Opinions

For boaters who used a launch, information on the conditions of their preferred launch can help state agencies assess maintenance or repairs needed for launch facilities.

Questions about whether the conditions needed to be improved at the boaters' preferred boat launch were asked in 2006 (Table 17). Sixty percent of freshwater boaters said launch facilities did not need improvements. Great Lakes boaters were even happier with their boat launch conditions; 66% claimed facilities did not need improvements. More than half (58%) of all saltwater boaters claimed their launch facilities did not need improvements.

For those boaters not satisfied with conditions of the facilities at their preferred boat launch, the launch ramp and restrooms were the most frequently mentioned facilities to need improvements. Forty-two percent of freshwater boaters expressed a need to repair launch ramps, 40% mentioned restroom facilities, and 28% reported parking lots at launch sites. Saltwater and Great Lakes boaters' expressed similar opinions about the launch ramps and restrooms needing improvements, although 15% or more of these boaters also reported "other" facilities as needing improvements.

Table 17. Boat Launch Facilities Improvement Opinions
(Population 16 years old and older. Numbers in thousands)

Boat Launch	Freshwater Boaters	Freshwater Percent	Great Lakes Boaters	Great Lakes Percent	Saltwater Boaters	Saltwater Percent
Total boat launch users	**7,601**	**100**	**615**	**100**	**2,461**	**100**
Facilities did not need improvements	4,574	60	403	66	1,430	58
Facilities that needed improvements:						
Launch ramp	1,270	42	*62	*15	389	38
Courtesy dock	623	21	...	...	222	22
Parking lot	860	28	*59	*15	302	29
Restroom facilities	1,196	40	*85	*21	377	37
Fish cleaning station	613	20	...	...	245	24
Potable water	378	12	...	...	175	17
Lights	555	18	...	...	155	15
Other facilities	368	12	*62	*15	202	20

*Estimate based on a sample size of 10–29.
... Sample size too small to report data reliably.
Note: Detail does not add to total because of multiple response and nonresponses.

Another way to examine where boating launch facility improvements are needed is to break down these requests by region. The following maps show which facility improvements are most important to users of boat launches in each U.S. Census division.[5]

The improvements mentioned continued to be restroom facilities and launch ramps. For freshwater boaters 46% or more in the New England, South Atlantic, and Pacific region said that restroom facilities needed improvements. This was higher than the national average of 40%. Between 46% and 52% of boaters in the West North Central, East South Central, West South Central, and Mountain responded that launch ramps needed to be improved, which was higher than the national average of 42%.

In the Pacific region 40% of saltwater boaters reported that fish cleaning stations needed improvements and 38% reported restroom facilities needed improvements. In the Mid-Atlantic, over two thirds of boaters reported no improvements necessary to their boat launches. In New England and the West South Central, parking lots and launch ramps were the two facilities needing the most improvement. The South Atlantic saltwater boaters mentioned launch ramps and restrooms as the two facilities needing the most improvements.

When the Great Lakes boaters were broken down by division, the only reportable results came from the East North Central. Here, launch ramps and restroom facilities ranked as the top two facilities that needed improvements.

---

[5] Please see the appendix for all boat launch facility improvement opinions by region.

Figure 7. Most Requested Freshwater Boat Launch Facility Improvements by Census Region

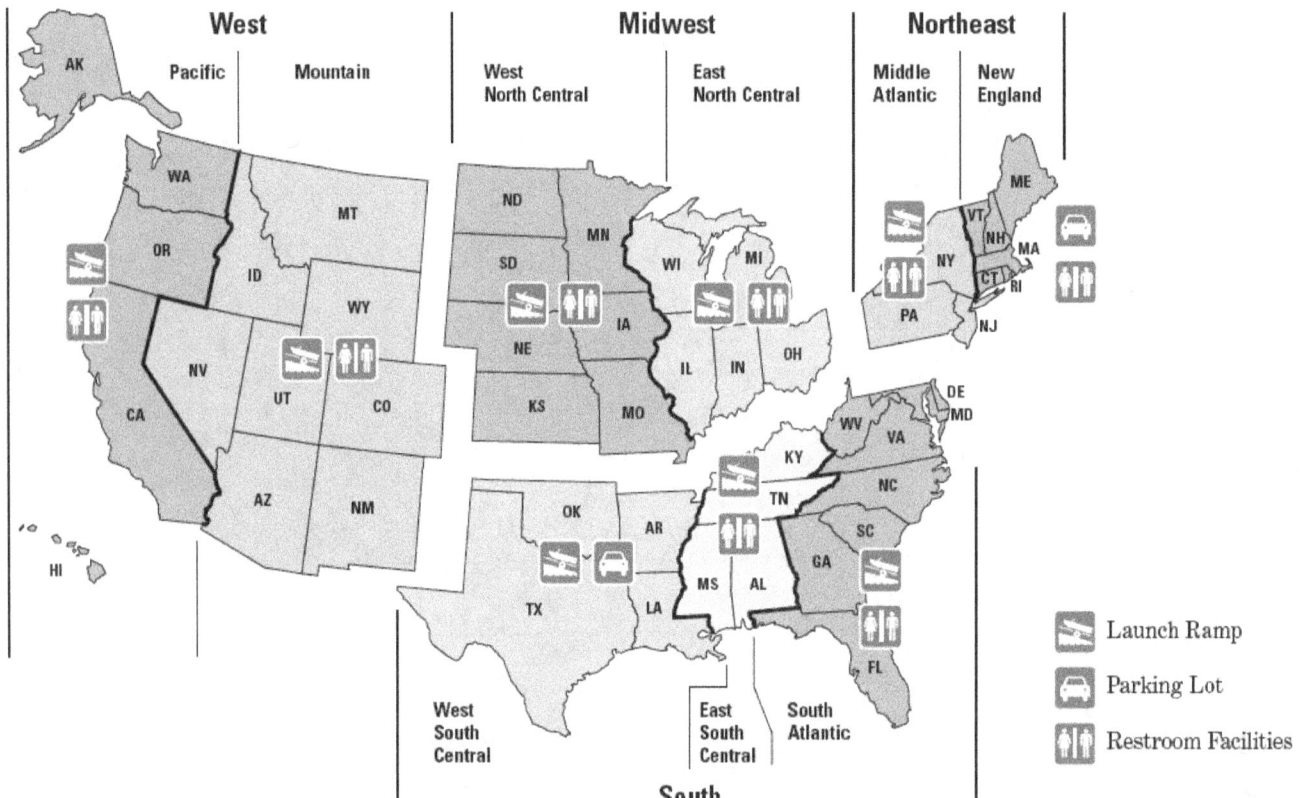

Figure 8. Most Requested Saltwater Boat Launch Facility Improvements by Census Region

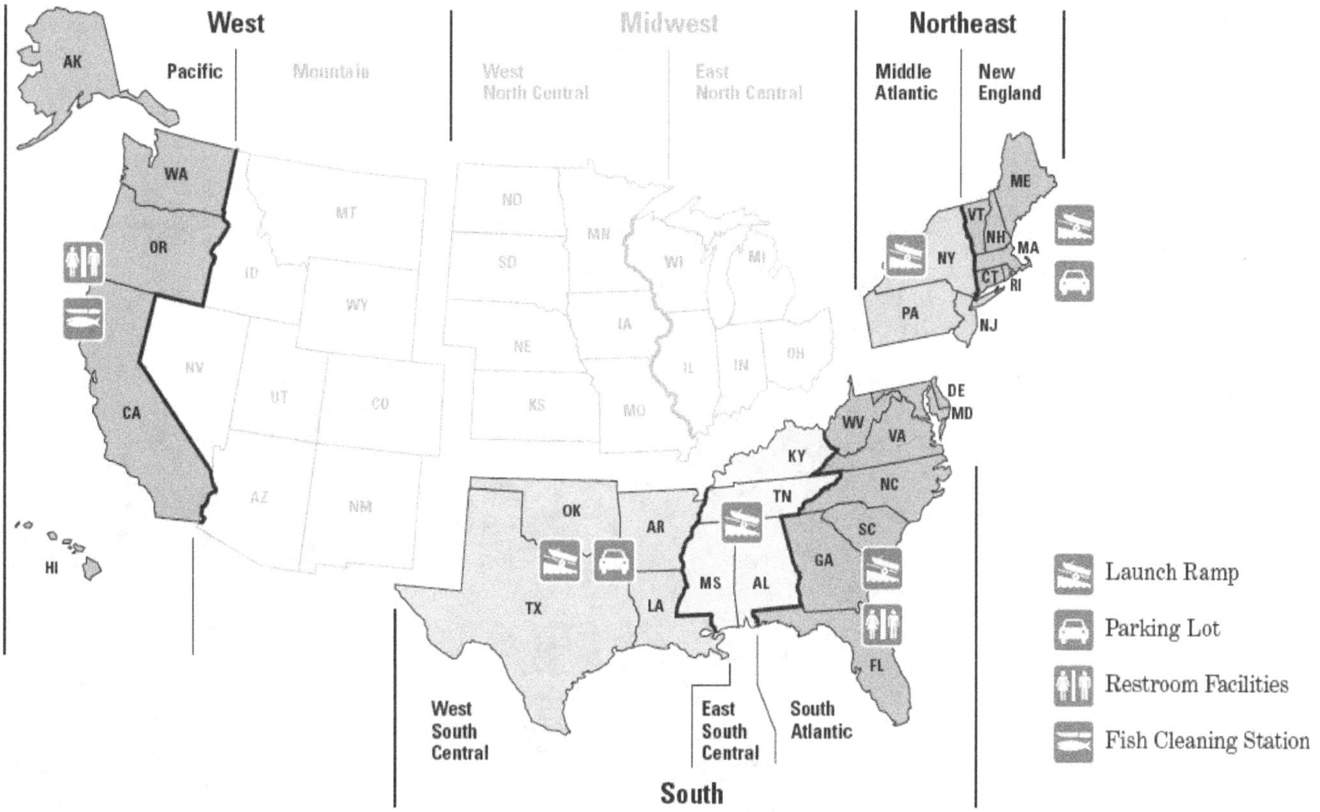

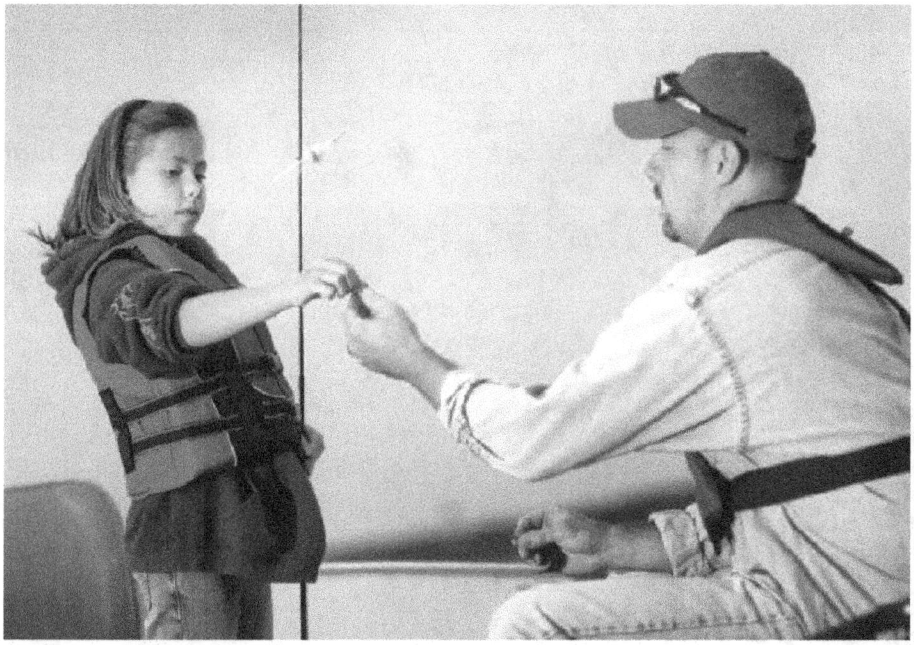

Courtesy of Take Me Fishing

Boater Expenditures

Freshwater boaters spent over $6 billion in 2006 on boats, accessories, rentals and more. This averaged $480 per angler. The motorboat, other than a bass boat, captured the most spending by freshwater boaters. Great Lakes boaters spent an average of $511 for a year of Great Lakes fishing. Saltwater anglers spent over $3 billion on boat rentals, equipment, and purchases in 2006. They had the highest per boater average with $596. Due to small sample sizes, expenditures for boat purchases are not reported separately for Great Lakes boaters.

Courtesy of Take Me Fishing

Table 18. Expenditures by Boaters for Freshwater, Great Lakes and Saltwater Fishing

Expenditure Item	Freshwater		Great Lakes		Saltwater	
	Amount (thousands of dollars)	Average per boater (dollars)	Amount (thousands of dollars)	Average per boater (dollars)	Amount (thousands of dollars)	Average per boater (dollars)
Total, all boating costs	**$6,276,419**	**$480**	**$538,291**	**$511**	**$3,160,113**	**$596**
Boat Rentals	$171,263	$13	$11,791	$11	$148,709	$28
Boat fuel	$1,013,385	$78	$135,212	$128	$643,136	$121
Boat launch fees	$84,562	$6	$13,530	$13	$36,055	$7
Depth finders, fish finders, and other electronic fishing devices	$246,138	$19	*$20,140	*$19	$175,771	$33
Other boating costs such as mooring, storage, maintenance, and pumpout fees	$663,797	$51	$146,329	$139	$628,398	$118
Boat Purchases						
Motorboat (other than bass boat)	$2,066,754	$158	...	...	$1,164,998	$220
Bass Boats	$1,590,640	$122	...	...	...	...
Canoes and other nonmotor boats	$68,739	$5	...	...	*$33,047	*$6
Boat motor, trailer or hitch and other boat accessories	$371,142	$28	...	...	$290,174	$55

*Estimate based on a sample size of 10–29.
... Sample size too small to report data reliably.

Conclusion

Seventeen million anglers (57% of all anglers) enjoyed recreational fishing from a boat in the United States in 2006. One million fished from a boat on the Great Lakes, 13 million in freshwater (other than the Great Lakes), and 5.3 million in saltwater. These anglers were primarily from urban areas, male, and middle aged.

Anglers fishing from a boat were most often accompanied by friends, but family members and spouses were also popular companions. In preparing for their trips, they mainly sought information on fish species, weather conditions, and fishing rules and regulations. They were most likely to get information from family, friends, or other boaters and anglers, as well as off the internet.

Motorboats were the most popular type of boat used, but the length preferred varied by type of water fished: freshwater anglers favored motorboats 13 to 16 feet long, while Great Lakes and saltwater anglers preferred 20- to 25-foot-long boats.

Fifty-eight percent of anglers used boat launches for access to the water for freshwater, non-Great Lakes fishing and for Great Lakes fishing in 2006. Saltwater anglers were less likely to use a boat launch, but the 46 % that did so did not travel as far to reach one. Sixty percent of the anglers that used boat launches reported that the facilities they used most often did not need improvements. Where they reported improvements needed, launch ramps and restrooms topped the list.

Courtesy of Take Me Fishing

Anglers spent a lot of money to fish from a boat in 2006. Almost $10 billion was spent on boats and related items purchased primarily for fishing, such as motors, trailers, fuel, launch fees, mooring, and storage. Great Lakes anglers fishing from a boat spent an average of $511 per person, freshwater (excluding Great Lakes) anglers spent $480 per person, and saltwater anglers spent $596 per person.

Boats provided access to areas far beyond the reach of shorelines and anglers will continue to use boats to reach their favorite fishing holes.

Appendix: Launch Facility Improvement Opinions by Census Region

The following three tables break down the boat launch facility improvement opinions by census region. Respondents were asked if any facilities at their preferred boat launch needed to be improved for more efficient use. A respondent had the flexibility to respond that none of the facilities needed improvements or if improvements were needed for more efficient use, a list of the boat launch facilities was read by the interviewer.

Courtesy of Take Me Fishing

Table A.1. Freshwater Boat Launch Facilities Improvement Opinions By Region
(Population 16 years old and older. Numbers in thousands)

	New England	Percent	Middle Atlantic	Percent	East North Central	Percent
Total boat launch users	248	100	404	100	1,470	100
Facilities did not need improvements	142	57	224	55	933	64
Facilities that needed improvements:						
Launch ramp	40	38	*76	*42	200	37
Courtesy dock	*26	*25	*26	*14	*102	*19
Parking lot	42	40	*44	*24	118	22
Restroom facilities	50	47	*61	*34	222	41
Fish cleaning station	*21	*20	...	...	*73	*14
Potable water	*20	*19	...	...	*35	*7
Lights	*21	*20	...	...	*84	*16
Other facilities	*17	*16	...	...	*49	*9

	West North Central	Percent	South Atlantic	Percent	East South Central	Percent
Total boat launch users	1,201	100	1,240	100	856	100
Facilities did not need improvements	714	60	725	58	541	63
Facilities that needed improvements:						
Launch ramp	221	46	185	36	164	52
Courtesy dock	116	24	107	21	*65	*21
Parking lot	157	32	150	29	103	33
Restroom facilities	165	34	246	48	129	41
Fish cleaning station	85	17	121	23	*50	*16
Potable water	*36	*7	*77	*15	*37	*12
Lights	70	14	86	17	93	30
Other facilities	49	10	*62	*12	*32	*10

	West South Central	Percent	Mountain	Percent	Pacific	Percent
Total boat launch users	896	100	581	100	706	100
Facilities did not need improvements	524	58	372	64	400	57
Facilities that needed improvements:						
Launch ramp	183	49	96	46	105	34
Courtesy dock	*79	*21	43	20	*60	*20
Parking lot	128	35	44	21	75	24
Restroom facilities	114	31	68	32	142	46
Fish cleaning station	104	28	43	21	97	32
Potable water	*48	*13	*23	*11	*73	*24
Lights	89	24	*29	*14	*49	*16
Other facilities	*47	*13	*45	*21	*56	*18

*Estimate based on a sample size of 10–29.
... Sample size too small to report data reliably.
Note: Detail does not add to total because of multiple response and nonresponses.

Table A.2. Saltwater Boat Launch Facilities Improvement Opinions By Region
(Population 16 years old and older. Numbers in thousands)

	New England	Percent	Middle Atlantic	Percent	South Atlantic	Percent
Total boat launch users	**149**	**100**	**198**	**100**	**900**	**100**
Facilities did not need improvements	80	54	122	62	507	56
Facilities that needed improvements:						
Launch ramp	*26	*38	41	54	123	31
Courtesy dock	*16	*23	...	...	*78	*20
Parking lot	*26	*38	...	...	92	23
Restroom facilities	*24	*35	...	...	167	42
Fish cleaning station	*12	*17	...	...	88	22
Potable water	*16	*23	...	...	78	20
Lights	*18	*26	...	...	*54	*14
Other facilities	*14	*20	...	...	*49	*12

	East South Central	Percent	West South Central	Percent	Pacific	Percent
Total boat launch users	**109**	**100**	**611**	**100**	**375**	**100**
Facilities did not need improvements	*57	*52	408	67	181	48
Facilities that needed improvements:						
Launch ramp	*24	*47	*86	*42	70	36
Courtesy dock	...	...	48	24	*40	*21
Parking lot	...	...	*86	*42	58	30
Restroom facilities	...	...	*73	*36	75	38
Fish cleaning station	...	...	39	19	77	40
Potable water	...	...	18	9	33	17
Lights	...	...	30	15	*26	*13
Other facilities	...	...	55	27	*39	*20

*Estimate based on a sample size of 10–29.
... Sample size too small to report data reliably.
Note: Detail does not add to total because of multiple response and nonresponses.

Table A.3. Great Lakes Boat Launch Facilities Improvement Opinions By Region
(Population 16 years old and older. Numbers in thousands)

	East North Central	Percent
Total boat launch users	**435**	**100**
Facilities did not need improvements	295	68
Facilities that needed improvements:		
Launch ramp	*46	*33
Courtesy dock	...	...
Parking lot	...	...
Restroom facilities	*51	*36
Fish cleaning station	...	...
Potable water	...	...
Lights	...	...
Other facilities	...	...

*Estimate based on a sample size of 10–29.
... Sample size too small to report data reliably.
Note: Detail does not add to total because of multiple response and nonresponses.

www.ingramcontent.com/pod-product-compliance
Lightning Source LLC
Chambersburg PA
CBHW052026280526
45793CB00005B/1145